WHAT'S UNDER ALL THOSE LEAVES?

Sally Zolkosky Labadie

Illustrated by Jeremiah

Sally Labadie
2015

Dedicated to **UNA,**
who loved all "critters,"
no matter how small.

Red, yellow, green and brown leaves cover the floor of the woods in autumn. The layer becomes deeper and deeper as more leaves fall.

WHAT'S UNDER ALL THOSE
LEAVES?
IS ANYTHING THERE?

Let's take a walk in the woods and see what we can find.

Red and black-spotted **LADYBUGS** have found a snug spot under the leaves where they can spend the cold winter. Huddled together they'll sleep until spring. When the coming snows melt and the air is warm, they'll crawl out and fly away to lay their eggs on new plants.

A gray field **MOUSE** is scurrying and sniffing to find seeds or berries to eat. Her whiskers quiver as she sniffs at the leaves. She'll take the food to her winter home in a hole in an old log so she won't have to go out in the snow. A gray mouse on the white snow would surely be seen by a hungry hawk or owl!

The bright red berries of the bearberry plant are just waiting to be dinner for a little animal. Will the field **MOUSE** find them? Maybe she already has some to put in her winter home.

Under the log where the soil stays moist a bluish-black spotted **SALAMANDER** lies quietly. See the yellow spots on her back and head? She will not wake until the warm spring rains come and the soil becomes soft, when she will crawl on her little legs to the pond to lay her eggs in the water.

In the forest above the logs stand tall oak, walnut and hickory trees. Many acorns, walnuts and hickory nuts fall onto leaves on the ground. If you listen you can hear the soft plunking sound of the nuts as they hit the leaves. **DEER** will come here during the winter and scrape away the snow with their hooves to find nuts to eat.

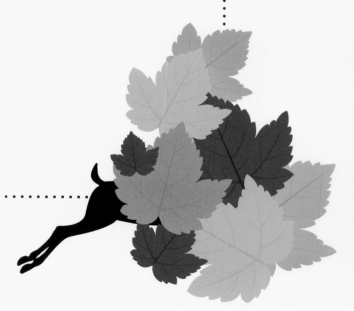

See the small burrow in the ground near the log? That's where a **CHIPMUNK** has made his winter home. He's a rusty brown color, with black and white stripes on his back and white around his eyes. He's been busy filling the burrow with walnuts and acorns so he'll have food to eat all winter. Watch him scurry back and forth with his jaws full of nuts. When he runs his fuzzy tail stands straight and tall.

A reddish-orange and brown fox **SQUIRREL** hurries around, carrying acorns, hickory nuts and walnuts to a hole in an old hickory tree so he can have food during the winter. He digs under the layer of leaves to bury another acorn as his fluffy tail twitches back and forth. He'll use his sense of smell to find it in the winter when he has eaten all the nuts in his tree. **SQUIRRELS** can find nuts they've buried, even under a blanket of snow.

Some of the nuts will stay buried in the ground and will grow into new walnut, hickory and oak trees. Do you think there is an animal who would like to eat the nuts from the new trees?

Under a layer of faded brown and green leaves
and moist brown dirt a striped forest **SNAIL**
sleeps tucked in his shell. The leaves and
dirt stay moist and make a warm bed for the
snail. He won't move until the ground warms in
the spring. The forest **SNAIL** does not live
in the water, but in the moist, rich earth.

A striped garter **SNAKE** is looking for a hole in the ground where he can sleep until spring. He slithers under the leaves and around fallen branches. Will he find the chipmunk hole? Will the chipmunk share the hole? The **SNAKE** disappears under the leaves as he glides silently away. He'll find another hole that is empty.

Leaves fall quietly onto a pile of old branches called a brush pile. Inside this brush pile lives a family of grayish brown cottontail rabbits. The RABBITS' "cottontail" is white, their feet are whitish, and they have orange fur behind their ears. The brush pile keeps them warm and protects them from animals looking for a RABBIT dinner. During the winter they will hop out to find green plants and grass that are hidden under the snow and leaves. The brush pile will be a safe place for the mother RABBIT to raise her babies in the spring.

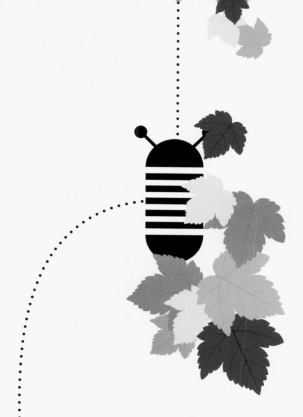

The brown and black woolly bear **CATERPILLAR** crawls quickly along. She's hoping to find a dry spot so she can sleep all winter. In the spring she'll make a cocoon and change into an Isabella moth. Maybe she'll find that hollow log. Do you think the mouse will let a little caterpillar join him?

There's another old log that is decomposing on the forest floor. Under the log is a tiny, dark gray bug all rolled up like a ball.

The **PILL BUG**, or roly-poly, lives in dark, damp places all year long feeding on the rotting wood. Near him is a small black **BEETLE** with horns, called a stag beetle. Both the pill bug and the beetle will sleep all winter until the plants start growing again. Then they'll suck the juice from the new plants and chew on the old log.

The red, yellow, green and brown leaves
make a thick carpet in the woods.

It's very quiet.

Now, can you answer the question

WHAT'S UNDER ALL THOSE
LEAVES?

 FriesenPress

Suite 300 - 990 Fort St
Victoria, BC, Canada, V8V 3K2
www.friesenpress.com

Copyright © 2015 by Sally Zolkosky Labadie
First Edition — 2015

Illustrations by Jeremiah

All rights reserved.

ISBN
978-1-4602-7583-2 (Paperback)
978-1-4602-7584-9 (eBook)

1. Juvenile Nonfiction, Science & Nature, Biology

Distributed to the trade by The Ingram Book Company

CPSIA information can be obtained
at www.ICGtesting.com
Printed in the USA
BVIC01n0639281015
423395BV00001B/2

9 781460 275832